Budging is Better

by Lexi Parker

Illustrations by Rose Bennington

For the families I've been lucky enough to work with.

Your effort, resilience, and love inspire me everyday.

More of your favorite characters from this series of books

Ralphie

Petey

Lana

Bob the banana slug lived in Slimy Slug Forest.
He shared his mossy log home with Mommy, Daddy, and Little Sister Slug.

He was a sweet slug who loved playing games like Slug Slide,
Giant Slime Splash, and Mud Pie Gobble.

But there was just one problem… Bob would not budge.
This meant that he wanted to do things the same way over and over again.

When it was Slug Slide time he always wanted the same friends to play.

One day Billy tried to join in on the fun, "Can I slide next?"
"Nope, no new comers allowed," blurted Bob. Bob would not budge.

Billy slid away crying. "Bob, please let Billy play too," said Mommy slug. "Sorry the game has to stay the same. "Bob would not budge.

When Bob was playing Giant Slime Splash, he wanted to play all by himself. "Can I splash too?" Little Sister begged. "Nope, you can only watch." Bob would not budge.

At dinner Bob made sure everyone ate the same mud pie and sat in the same spot. One night Daddy changed dinner by adding some moss to the mud pie. "I'm not eating this!" Bob pouted. He would not budge.

Daddy was tired of Bob not budging and refused to give him his usual mud pie. Bob slid off to his hole to sleep. He was very hungry.

The next morning Bob slid out to go play Slug Slide with his buddies, but when he arrived no one was there.

He slid all around and found them at a new hill.
"Hey what's going on?" asked Bob. "Sorry Bob, but we wanted Billy to play too. Since you won't budge, we had to find a new hill to slide down."

Bob turned around ready to leave, but then he remembered
how sad he was the night before when he ended up hungry because
he would not budge.

Not wanting to miss out on the fun again, Bob decided that maybe he could try to budge this time. "Can I play too?" Bob asked. "Of course," his friends happily exclaimed.

Bob sludged up the new hill. He took a deep breath and…

"Whooooo!"
This hill was even faster!
'Maybe budging wasn't so bad after all,' thought Bob.

Later that day Bob was playing Giant Slime Splash.
"Can I play too?" asked Little Sister Slug. Bob was about to say no when he
thought about how much fun budging had been during slug slide.
"Sure, come on in." They counted down together "3,2,1," and jumped up to...

SPLASH!
This splash was the biggest splash Bob had ever made.
'Wow, budging is definitely more fun,' thought Bob.

At dinner, Bob sat in a different spot. "Um, Bob.
Do you know that's a different spot?" asked Mommy.
"Yep, I'm budging today!"

That night the banana slug family had an extra long cuddle because they were so proud of Bob for budging. "So, is budging better?" asked Daddy. "Yes," giggled Bob. "Budging is definitely better."

THE END

www.ingramcontent.com/pod-product-compliance
Lightning Source LLC
Chambersburg PA
CBHW041243040426
42445CB00004B/133